True Chameleons
Part II Notes on Popular Species
Diseases and Disorders
by Philippe de Vosjoli

Table of Contents

Introduction

This book was written as a companion to *The General Care and Maintenance of True Chameleons Part 1: Husbandry.*

The first part of this book presents notes gathered by the author on various chameleon species over several years. For the purpose of this book, the notes were loosely organized and allowed to remain in the abbreviated style in which they were originally written. A primary goal of these notes is to offer guidelines for the selection and general care of some of the most readily available chameleon species at the time of writing. The information presented was the result of personal experience, research of the literature and conversations with other herpetoculturists. Little information has been presented in these notes regarding the breeding of chameleons. This area is literally in its infancy and not enough information was available at the time of writing to cover this subject in a satisfactory manner. A third book, Part 3, will be published on the captive breeding of true chameleons at the end of 1991.

The second part of this book deals with diseases and disorders in chameleons. It was written from the point of view of a herpetoculturist with the goals of presenting an overview of the health problems commonly encountered in chameleons and to assist herpetoculturists in making decisions regarding veterinary treatment.

A Word of Advice

Before tackling new or difficult species, acquire some experience with chameleon species known to be relatively easy to maintain in captivity. If you want to work with live-bearing highland species, begin with Jackson's chameleons *(C. jacksoni)* or the mountain dwarf chameleons*(C. bitaeniatus and C. ellioti)* before setting out to work with high-casqued chameleons *(C. hohnelii)*. If you are interested in working with egg-laying species, start with panther chameleons *(C. pardalis)* or Oustalet's chameleon (*C. oustaleti*) or *C. johnstoni* before working with *C. gracilis* or *C. brevicornis* . Initial successes in maintenance will provide rewards which will encourage you to pursue working with true chameleons. Beginning with difficult species such as *C. gracilis* and *C. senegalensis* can quickly lead to discouragement that may have you give up on chameleons altogether. **YOU HAVE TO BE A BEGINNER BEFORE BECOMING AN EXPERT.**

Things to consider before getting involved with chameleons.

1. If you are not committed and involved with the animals, let them fall into better hands.

2. Don't believe for a minute that you're an expert or better than the next person. Just when you think you've got it, you don't. There is always something you can learn even from the amateur who doesn't brag about being an expert.

3. If you're not an expert you won't be able to save those so-so or sickly chameleons at an importer or pet store. Experts usually can't save them. Instead of thinking about saving poor chameleons, you're better off thinking about saving your money.

4.   Acquire experience with the "easier" species before trying to tackle and "solve" the more difficult ones.

5.   Before working with a given species, ask yourself whether you are actually able to provide the right conditions to maintain it. A common error is working with montane/highland species without being willing to incorporate expensive cooling systems into their household.

6.   Don't overdiversify. Stick to just a few species and follow them to the desired end; multiple generation propagation of chameleons in captivity.

7.   Have animals checked for bacterial and parasite infections, then treat them.

8.   Even in the midst of apparent slaughter, don't give up. Perseverance is the key to success. If you start off with healthy animals and you fail repeatedly, then modify your conditions. You're doing something wrong or the animal is stressed or has a disease that you haven't noticed or treated.

9.   Keep notes of your progress and keep records of your animals and the vivarium conditions under which they were maintained. Later, the keys to probable success may be in those notes.

So *Chamaeleo species* x did well for so many months and all of a sudden looked a little off and started going downhill. What changed? Was there a heat wave? A cooling trend? A drop in relative air humidity? Did you switch diets?

Notes on Chameleon Species

Female flap-necked chameleon (*Chamaeleo dilepis*). This animal had to be held because it was so restless.

FLAP-NECKED CHAMELEON
(Chamaeleo dilepis):

Wide-ranging, tropical and South Africa. Size: Some populations up to nearly 13 inches. Sexing: Females as large as males and heavier bodied. Males have visible hemipenile bulges. This is a very nervous and aggressive species which readily becomes stressed. As with all other species, does best when obtained at smaller sizes. Animals are sometimes so nervous that they will not readily feed in front of an observer. Treat animals for parasites. Some groups come in with subcutaneous nematodes. Best treated as a tropical climate chameleon but will safely tolerate night drops into the 60's. Should be provided with plant shelters. A wide ranging species with variation in size and degree of "flap" development among populations. Best kept singly outside of breeding attempts. If healthy when obtained, many animals tend to do quite well. Captive longevity at least three years. Egg-laying, 25-40 eggs.

Gravid female Senegal chameleon.

SENEGAL CHAMELEON *(Chamaeleo senegalensis):*

The most frequently imported chameleon and one of the least recommended. Sexing: males more slender bodied than females. Males have clearly visible hemipenile bulges. Following administration of a wormer, they can manifest varying degrees of subcutaneous bleeding as well as internal bleeding. Some groups of imports have numerous subcutaneous nematodes. Generally does poorly in part because of heavy parasite loads that contributes to its decline. Longevity in captivity, 2-1/2 years plus. In the wild, lifespan probably under 2-1/2 years. Massive die-outs in the wild are said to be common with this species as with several other egg laying species. Drought is a contributing factor in die-outs of adults. Next generation is found in eggs underground during these drought periods. Smaller specimens are recommended for long-term success with this species. These small specimens should be checked and treated for parasites. Generally a rather nervous species which may refuse to feed when observers are present. It does best in vivaria with some plantings. Requires daytime temperatures up to 85F but relatively tolerant of temperature drops at night into the 50's. Possibly captive hatched or bred animals may adapt better to captivity. Not a good choice for first time chameleon owners who will be tempted by the low cost but disappointed and discouraged by the poor survival of this species. Egg-laying, up to 80 eggs.

GRACEFUL CHAMELEON *(Chamaeleo gracilis):*

This is a typically parasite-loaded species that does not usually adjust well to captivity. What has been said about *C. senegalensis* pretty much applies for this species. Egg-laying.

Male Johnston's chameleon.

JOHNSTON'S CHAMELEON *(Chamaeleo johnstoni):*

Most imported specimens are from Burundi, Africa. Size: Up to 11 inches. Sexing: Males have three horns. Females lack horns. Females have bright yellow-orange to orange markings around lower jaw area. In appearance, resembles a slender-bodied but more colorful *C. jacskoni.* Unlike *C. jacksoni,* this species requires daytime temperatures of 85F and can tolerate up to 92F. At 95F, signs of heat stress become apparent including drastic lightening of body coloration and gaping. Nighttime temperatures should be in the 70's. Very low nighttime temperatures may be detrimental.

C.johnstoni usually does not harbor subcutaneous nematodes but will have nematodes and other parasites in G.I. tract. Protozoan infections are common among imported animals. *Trichomonas* and *Giardia* have been found in stool checks. Respiratory infections are also common in imports. The cause of these infections has yet to be determined. Mucus in mouth and a wheeze which can be felt by applying a finger gently against the side of the throat are simple means of diagnosis. One probable cause in captivity is the misinformation that this species has requirements similar to Jackson's chameleons resulting in their being kept at temperatures that are too cool. In large vivaria, *C. johstoni* can be kept in groups of one male and several females; otherwise best kept singly. Adaptability to captivity is variable depending on groups of imports. Animals from healthy groups tend to do well in captivity and have proven quite hardy. On the other hand other, a group of these will come in and most of the animals from that group will start to decline though they may have initially appeared to be healthy. Egg-laying: 6-16 eggs per clutch. A very promising species.

Close-up of female Jackson's chameleon.

JACKSON'S CHAMELEON *(Chamaeleo jacksoni)*:

East Africa. Size: up to 13 inches. Sexing: Males same size as females. Males have three horns on head. Females sometimes have a diminutive horn on snout. Horn stubs visible in male hatchlings. Initially, most imported specimens were from East Africa but currently most imported animals originate from Hawaii where this species was introduced. For long-term availability, field culture in Hawaii should be considered. Relatively few animals are produced and successfully raised in captivity. Some of the best captive breeding results have been by herpetoculturists in Southern California coastal areas where this species can be maintained outdoors year round.

This species has been kept and bred in captivity for several generations both in the U.S. and Europe. In a mixed collection, all new specimens must be quarantined a long distance from original group. Other species of chameleons should also be quarantined from established groups of *C. jacksoni*. A probable chameleon virus, apparently airborne, if introduced can decimate a captive group of *C. jacksoni*.

A high altitude species in the wild. Fares best when kept as a montane/ highland species. Should be maintained at temperatures of 75-85F during the day with marked temperature drop at night. Adults will tolerate temperature drops to near freezing but daytime exposure to sunlight and higher temperatures are a must. Relative air humidity of 50-60% is recommended with good ventilation. Longevity in captivity, eight years plus. Can be kept in pairs in larger enclosures. Live bearing. Gestation around three months. Juveniles can be difficult to rear. They have a very low tolerance for stress and neglect. Transport or shipping of juveniles not recommended until at least two inches snout to vent length. Rearing juveniles singly may increase success. Feeding week old crickets and wingless fruit flies two to three times a day is recommended. Insects should be nutrient-loaded and vitamin/mineral supplemented. Adults will feed on a variety of insects and also on small land snails. When rearing juveniles, the faster the growth rate (dependent on feeding schedule and temperature range), the greater the probability of successful rearing. Juveniles should not be exposed to the extremes of temperature that adults are capable of tolerating. Recommend 80F daytime and 60F minimum nighttime temperature for rearing of juveniles. Sexual maturity is reached in under two years.

Gravid female two-lined chameleon.

TWO-LINED CHAMELEON *(Chamaeleo bi-taeniatus):*

East Africa. Size: 6-8 inches. Sexing: Sexes similar in size. Females are heavier bodied than males. Look for hemipenile bulges in males. This species has been bred over several generations in Europe. A low elevation, highland species that should be maintained like *C. jacksoni.* Will show signs of heat stress at 90F. Minimum night temperature 50F.

Can be housed in pairs. This is a relatively hardy species. Should be treated for parasites. Live-bearing. Juveniles are very small but relatively easy to rear. Sexual maturity reached by one year.

MOUNTAIN DWARF CHAMELEON
(Chamaeleo ellioti):

Part of the *C. bitaeniatus* complex. *C. ellioti* is more slender bodied, with linear patterns running the length of the body and more colorful than C. bitaeniatus. Northern populations have distinct deep throat grooves lined in black. Southern populations may lack the black but retain deep throat grooves. Northern population males can have a turquoise background color. This is one of the most attractive of live-bearing chameleons. This species inhabits dry savannahs at lower elevations of the highlands. Can be raised like *C. bitaeniatus*. Live-bearing.

Male, southern form of C. ellioti.

11

HIGH-CASQUED CHAMELEON

(Chamaeleo hoehnelii):
Once imported in large numbers out of Kenya but now seldom available. Size: 6-8 inches. Sexing: Males larger than females. Males have a high helmet compared to females. Adult males much more colorful than females often with turquoise and orange. A montane/highland species which should be maintaine d like *C. jacksoni.* Has been successfully maintained and bred in Europe for several generations. Best kept in single pairs. Live-bearing. Juveniles very small and a challenge to rear.

COMMON CHAMELEON *(Chamaeleo chamaeleon ssp):*

Specimens available in the U.S. are primarily from Egypt and Israel. At the time of writing no imports were available. Size: Up to 11 inches. When available this is a species which oftens adapts well to captivity after treatment for parasites. Requires high daytime temperatures but tolerates temperature drops into the 40's at night. Very asocial. Outside of brief introductions for breeding, both sexes should be kept separately. Requires a cooling period of 6-8 weeks for pre-breeding conditioning (temperatures in the 50's and 60's). Egg-laying.

Failed breeding attempt by panther chameleons.

Male "blue phase" panther chameleon from Nossi Be.

PANTHER CHAMELEON *(Chamaeleo pardalis):*

Madagascar and the islands of Mauritius and Reunion (introduced). Size: Males up to 20 inches. Females usually under 13 inches. Sexing: Males much larger than females. Males have a more developed helmet. Males are very variable in color. Some forms are turquoise (many from Nossi Be), others are green with varying amounts of red, some have extensive orange, some have bright cobalt blue spotting. Females of some forms have very attractive peach-orange coloration. Females much more nervous and reclusive than males. One of the best adapted chameleons for indoor keeping. Must be treated for parasites. Imported males fare well but imported females often do not. These chameleons harbor large numbers of parasites including subcutaneous nematodes (particularly females). Captive longevity in males, eight years plus. Quite a few babies were hatched in captivity in the U.S. in 1989 and 1990. Egg-laying: clutch sizes 20 and up. Produces multiple clutches within a breeding season. Recommended incubation temperature 80-82F. Juveniles are best raised singly. Adults can be kept in pairs or trios in very large

in herpetoculture and will probably be the first species to be produced on a commercial scale. Males of this species are probably the best choice for anyone wishing to own a single chameleon as a pet. Best choice for an indoor species.

Close-up of head of female Parson's chameleon

PARSON'S CHAMELEON *(Chamaeleo parsoni):*

Madagascar. Size: Up to nearly two feet. One of the largest and most spectacular species of chameleons. Sexing: Males are larger than females. Males have enlarged and projecting ornaments above and in front of the nostrils. Color in males is also different than that of females. Adult males have a turquoise to aqua coloration and can adopt a pattern with reddish to orange crossbands. The eyelids are a bright yellow-orange. Females are typically green with a single bright yellow spot on each side. They can adopt a pattern with dark crossbands. The eyelids are yellow. These chameleons must be treated for parasites and can be difficult to acclimate. Compared to other chameleon species, Parson's chameleons are so sluggish that people have described them as "the sloth of the chameleons". This species doesn't tolerate extremes of heat or cold. Best kept at 80-85F during the daytime. Night temperature should not drop below 65F.

Needs high relative air humidity. A misting system is recommended for animals in large displays. Needs lots of water. Newly imported specimens can be reluctant to feed on crickets but will feed on larger grasshoppers, king mealworms *(Zoophobias)* and cockroaches. Occasional hand feeding of fuzzy mice recommended. Some end up taking mice on their own. Not yet captive-bred but well worth every expense and effort to do so. Probably very long lived. Overall not very tolerant of stress. Egg-laying: 25 or more eggs per clutch. Females are often weakened after egg-laying and need to be given regular attention to rehydrate and to hand feed until back in condition. Egg retention by females because of unsuitable egg-laying site is a cause of decline and death. To date, there have been no successful hatchings of this species in captivity. The author has opened a number of eggs laid by imported females and did not see any signs of fertility, such as presence of blood vessels or developing embryos. The shell on the eggs of *C. parsoni* is extremely tough and the author suspects that special conditions are required for successful hatching. This species, once established, is a good choice for maintaining indoors.

OUSTALET'S CHAMELEON *(Chamaeleo oustaleti):*

Madagascar. Size: Up to two feet. Sexing: Females smaller than males. Females do not have the raised helmet of males. As with most chameleon species, females more nervous. Males have slight hemipenile bulges posterior to the vent. Adult males have extensive red coloration, particularly in breeding. Relatively few females imported compared to males. This species and Parson's chameleon are the largest chameleons. This is a shy, nervous chameleon which often adapts well to captivity.

Chamaeleo oustaleti requires high temperatures, 85-90 F during the day, and moderate temperatures, 70-75F at night. Must be treated for parasites, particularly nematodes, a repeated number of times. It prefers dead branches as resting sites over planted areas. It appears to be arid adapted and does not require as much humidity and water as other species. Prefers crickets and grasshoppers as food items but will also take king mealworms. Adults can be hand-fed pink or fuzzy mice. Requires large amounts of food. Not very agressive. In a large enclosure more than one pair can be kept together but must be monitored during the breeding season.

C. oustaleti has been successfully bred at the Oklahoma City Zoo. Their hatch rate was low because optimal parameters for incubation have yet to be determined. The chameleons that did hatch, however, have proven hardy and presented no unusual problems in rearing. Sexual maturity can be reached within eighteen months and females multiple clutch. More work should be done to establish this promising species in herpetoculture. Egg-laying.

Young adult male Oustalet's chameleon.

Male *Chamaeleo verrucosus.* Note the enlarged scales on the side of the head compared to *C. oustaleti.*

MADAGASCAR GIANT CHAMELEON
(Chamaeleo verrucosus):

Madagascar. Size: Up to 23 inches. Males larger than females. Males have raised helmets. Hemipenile bulges are clearly visible in males. Can be distinguished from Oustalet's chameleon by the enlarged scales on the sides of the head. This species has faded green in it's coloration. Can be maintained like *C. oustaleti* but more *t*olerant of cooler temperatures. Appears to adapt well after inital acclimation. Adult males are very impressive. In terms of both looks and personality, this is one of the author's favorite species. Egglaying.

CARPET OR JEWEL CHAMELEON
(Chamaeleo lateralis):

Madagascar. Size: 5 - 7 1/2 inches. When available, these are sold as carpet chameleons. Males larger than females and more colorful. Males are asocial and agressive; they are best kept singly. This is a very attractive species which can adopt colors and patterns that include pastel blues, oranges, reds and yellows. This is a variable species with populations inhabiting a variety of habitats. Imported specimens are best maintained as standard tropical chameleons with a marked drop in night temperatures. Will tolerate night drops into the 50's. Day/night temperature fluctuations are recommended. Long-term maintenance in the U.S. has not been very successful. Bustard in England, however, considers this to be an easy species to maintain. This should be a good candidate for indoor maintenance and propagation once some of the problems have been resolved. Egg-laying.

Rearing hatchling/newborn chameleons

1. Place chameleons in small vivaria.
2. Raising chameleons singly leads to a better survival rate.
3. Landscape with thin stemmed branches and/or live plants.
4. Offer twice a day pinhead to one week old crickets or wingless fruitflies coated with a mix of 50% powdered reptile vitamin and 50% calcium carbonate or OsteoForm®.
5. Mist two to three times daily. Juvenile chameleons dehydrate quickly.
6. Allow exposure to diffused sunlight (i.e. through shade cloth or through dense leaves of plants) for several hours each week. **Warning: Hatchling or juvenile chameleons will quickly roast if kept in direct sunlight on a hot day. Don't place a glass-sided vivarium containing juveniles in direct sunlight.**
7. Keep at moderate temperatures within adult range require ments. Avoid extremes of heat or cold.

Diseases and Disorders

At the onset, herpetoculturists should be forewarned that diseases in true chameleons are difficult to treat successfully. As a rule, by the time a chameleon manifests symptoms of disease that are noticeable to the human eye, the disease will often have progressed to the point where the prognosis for successful recovery is poor. Thus, it is imperative that chameleons be kept under optimal conditions, be checked out by a knowledgeable and experienced reptile veterinarian for internal parasites and other possible causes of disease **BEFORE** obvious symptoms become apparent. With chameleons, prevention is critical. With most species of chameleons, once an animal appears obviously sick, chances of it surviving are poor and one must carefully consider whether the costs of veterinary treatment are warranted when the probability of recovery is relatively small. Such factors as cost of animal, rarity of animal and severity of symptoms must be considered. Before going to a veterinarian, set a budget limit for yourself. Remember, most obviously sick chameleons taken to veterinarians end up dying. If the symptoms are mild and the animal is not too listless or off feed or too emaciated, the chances for recovery are somewhat increased.

The following information is provided to aid herpetoculturists in assessing the health of their animals and in making decisions regarding veterinary treatment. The information is presented in terms that will render it useful for laymen and is not intended as source material for veterinarians. Nonetheless some of the information (presented from the point of view of a herpetoculturist) may be of assistance in helping veterinarians diagnose some of the special problems associated with chameleons.

DAILY MONITORING OF CHAMELEONS:

Chameleons should be checked daily to establish their state of health. The earliest symptoms of stress or disease are inactivity, listlessness, loss of weight and loss of appetite. If any of these symptoms are noticed then one should proceed as quickly as possible to determine what may be wrong and attempt to remedy it. If delayed, any disease or problem will very likely get worse and you will lose your animal(s).

NOTE WITH REGARDS TO HANDLING:

Chameleons have very strong jaw muscles and care must be used when examining the inside of the mouth of chameleons. The inexperienced use of instruments to keep the mouth open or when treating the mouth, can result in injury and, if stomatitis is present, in lower jaw fracture.

NOTE WITH REGARD TO ORAL ADMINISTRATION OF FLUIDS:

Any fluids administered orally should be administered in small amounts. There is a risk of fluids entering the lungs if administered in too large an amount. When administering liquids, a soft disposable eye-dropper should be used.

"SUNKEN EYES" SYNDROME:

Chameleons that are obviously sick eventually develop "sunken eyes", combined with inactivity and long periods of resting with closed eyes. The "sunken eyes" syndrome is apparently caused by overall weakness and the resulting loss of muscle tone. Chameleons which demonstrate this syndrome are ill and not very likely to survive.

STRESS

It seems fitting that in a section dealing with diseases and disorders of chameleons we should first address the question of stress. For the most part, chameleons are specialized lizards with varying abilities to adapt to the captive environment. If the environmental and social conditions are inadequate, chameleons will experience stress. With prolonged stress, feeding eventually stops, the immune system will become depressed, the susceptibility to disease will increase and a harmful physiological stress syndrome will set in. With all species of chameleons, careful observation will be required to determine the level of stress.

Some species are so aggressive and asocial that placing a group of these together in a small vivarium will result in all of them demonstrating varying signs of social stress with an unusual degree of frequency. The author observed this recently when visiting a dealer's set up containing several specimens of the veiled chameleon (*Chamaeleo calyptratus*). Specimens at various times would display, with high frequency to conspecifics, flattening their bodies and gaping. But the crowded conditions and small cage left them with no room to escape. The social stress level was constant and many specimens appeared to be ill. Observation should allow you to determine the social tolerance of a given species of chameleon. If the chameleon species is asocial, keep animals separately and create barriers so that they cannot see each other.

Some chameleons are so nervous in the presence of an observer that they will adopt a defensive display and refuse to feed or drink if anyone is nearby. Here again, a system must be devised to allow for watering and feeding without exposure to an observer.

Regarding enviromental stress, if one does some research on their animal's country of origin, habitat and climate, then it should be possible to design a vivarium which offers the desirable range of conditions for some degree of self regulation, i.e., being able to get away from the "hot spot" under the spotlight and into the shaded area of the vivarium. A rule of thumb is that when you don't have adequate information, create a vivarium with a range of climatic and landscape opportunities and observe the behavior of the animal.

It is critical that you address the question of stress as a first step toward dealing with and treating any disease or disorder.

EXTERNAL PARASITES

True chameleons do not readily harbor external parasites. However, some eye problems in chameleons are caused by the presence of mites between the rims of the eyelids and the eye itself. If looked at carefully, a small space will be seen between the eyelid and eye. Usually mites are not noticed until the eye(s) remain shut because they have developed an infection. Earlier symptoms include frequent rubbing of the eye(s) against branches.

A cotton swab, dipped in water or in an ophthalmic solution, gently run between the closed eyelids, will often remove a number of mites which then will confirm their presence. Check the rest of your collection to make sure that mites are not present on other lizards (the usual source of introduction of mites in a chameleon collection).

Treatment:

The treatment of mites in chameleons is somewhat difficult. A simple method is to use a cotton swab dipped in an ophthalmic solution and remove mites until they are no longer present. The use of insecticidal powders or sprays is out of the question since the mites tend to be lodged against the eye. The use of Vapona® impregnated pest strips,

21

as is recommended for snakes, can be dangerous and is not recommended with chameleons. One possible alternative which will have to be explored is to use the wormer Ivermectin® which has proven to be effective for killing mites. But mites will usually be present in the vivarium and surrounding areas and depending on the type of vivarium employed, mites can be difficult to completely exterminate. If the vivarium is a glass aquarium, it can be thoroughly cleaned with a chlorine solution and rinsed out. The surrounding area should be treated with a pyrethrin spray. If the vivarium is a screened enclosure, the chameleon(s) should be taken out. The enclosure should be wrapped in plastic and treated with Vapona® impregnated insect strips.

Ticks:

Recently, the author has seen a number of imported dwarf chameleons, primarily *Chamaeleo ellioti* and some *C. bitaeniatus* with numerous tiny ticks embedded in the axillary (arm-pit) area, inguinal area (thigh-body joint) and in the legs. Several animals had over 50 embedded ticks in these areas. It is not clear whether these ticks were initially present in the imported animals or whether they were contracted at the holding compound or importer.

Treatment: A pyrethrin solution on a cotton swab should be applied to infected areas. Later the ticks should be removed carefully with tweezers.

INTERNAL PARASITES

This was covered in the previously published book on chameleon husbandry. If you are serious about what you are doing, you will have cultures and tests done and administer the appropriate treatment. What else is there to say. **Recommended parasiticides and dosages are as follows:**

For NEMATODES (roundworms)

Fenbendazole, 75mg/kg, orally. Repeat in two weeks. May have to be repeated.

Or

Levamisole hydrochloride, 10mg/kg, orally. Repeat intwo weeks.

Or

Thiabendazole, 75mg/kg, orally. Repeat in two weeks.

For CESTODES (tapeworms)

Niclosamide, 150mg /kg, orally. Repeat in two weeks.

For PROTOZOAN parasites

Metronidazole at 100mg/kg, orally. Repeat in two weeks.

WORMS under the skin

Some imported chameleons come in with long coiled worms clearly visible under the skin. These should be avoided. Often, purchased animals which initially did not have apparent worms under the skin later may manifest them. When the subcutaneous masses appear as lumps without clear definition of the worm body, these worms are usually plerocercoid tapeworms in which the chameleon acts as an intermediate host for the worm to complete its life cycle. Typically, one stage of worm is ingested along with prey by a chameleon. The immature stages of the worm develop inside the chameleon and then migrate to an area beneath the skin presumably to be ingested by a chameleon predator which fills another intermediate role in the worm cycle. However, most subcutaneous worms in chameleons often demonstrate a well defined body outline under the skin. Upon removal, these appear to be large nematodes which have migrated beneath the skin. Many species such as *C. senegalensis* and *C. dilepis* and female *C. pardalis* can harbor large numbers of these worms. Treatment will require two people (one to hold the chameleon and one to remove worm) and involve, first removing any worms near the skin surface through a small incision (1/8" - 1/4") carefully performed after disinfecting the area incised and the instrument used. Extreme

23

care must be taken to only incise the skin just above where a worm is present. Once incised, the worm will appear as a whitish mass which can be carefully removed with tweezers. No more than one or two worms should be removed at a time to prevent injury and the possibility of trauma to the animal. Repeat treatment to remove other worms in one or two weeks. Once all worms are removed, treat the animal with a suitable wormer such as Fenbendazole. Prognosis will depend on many factors, particularly the number of worms present.

Subcutaneous nematodes in female panther chameleon.

MOUTHROT OR STOMATITIS

Look for any signs of this before you buy a chameleon. Most imported chameleons, when picked up, have a typical gaping behavior whereby the mouth is threateningly opened. Look inside for the presence of any unusual swelling and/or the presence of areas with caseous matter (yellowish or whitish "cheesy" looking matter). This is a typical characteristic of a bacterial infection generally known as stomatitis. If present in an animal you are about to purchase, return the animal to its cage and make another selection.

Regular inspection of the mouth during gaping responses should be made with the animals in one's collection. Other symptoms of mouthrot include swelling of the "gumline", a mouth that doesn't close completely and eventually, loss of appetite. If untreated the animal will invariably die, usually as a result of an infection which eventually destroys bone and frequently results in lower jaw fracture.

When the upper jaw is affected, stomatitis can result in infraorbital infections and upper jaw necrosis.

Treatment

Treat the infected area daily either with Betadine® or hydrogen peroxide. Extreme care must be given during treatment not to put pressure on jaws (i.e., trying to open mouth) or to allow the chameleon to bite down on a tool used to apply medication. Use only flexible instruments and try to elicit gaping behavior to get the chameleon to open its mouth. Ideally, an injectable antibiotic should also be used. Once the lower jaw is fractured, prognosis is poor. Vitamin C should be administered during the course of treatment. Also vitamin C in a pulverized powdered form or through oranges fed to food items is recommended for preventive measures.

MOUTH JUNCTURE INFECTIONS

For reasons which are not very clear, chameleons may develop infections at the mouth juncture. When a chameleon opens its mouth, this will be **visible as the fleshy area where the two jaws meet**. Chameleons will sometimes accumulate a certain amount of crud or caseous matter in this area. In some cases the area swells and becomes infected. If untreated, it can lead to infraorbital infections. This area should be examined, cleaned and disinfected with Betadyne solution if any caseous matter begins to accumulate.

Mouth juncture of female panther chameleon .

INFRAORBITAL INFECTIONS

Infraorbital infections are often the result of a spreading infection that begins in the upper jaw as stomatitis (mouthrot) or of an infection at the mouth juncture. Symptoms typically consist of pronounced swelling of the area under an eye. Treatment of the infection will usually be performed from the initially infected areas (e.g., the upper jaw). These types of infections require drainage followed by flushing with Betadine® and antibiotic therapy.

EYE INFECTIONS

Eye infections can have multiple causes. In some species of chameleons they tend to occur more frequently than in others. Mites between the rim of the eye and the eye itself may play a role in some infections. Diet and vitamins A and C may play a role in preventing infections. Typical symptoms of eye infections consist of first keeping one eye closed and later closing both eyes. If the eyelid is opened, the cornea will appear clouded. The rims of the eyelids may appear swollen. Ideally, treatment would require a culture by a veterinarian to determine effective antibiotics. Prognosis is not always very good for chameleons with eye infections, possibly because the susceptibility to infection is a sign that the chameleon is affected by other diseases.

INFECTED TONGUE

This will be noticed in cases where a chameleon can no longer project its tongue or only project it a short distance. Frequently, chameleons with an infected tongue go off feed or fail to catch insect prey. Examination of the tongue during gaping will reveal that it is swollen and reddish. Treating orally with tetracycline at a dosage of 5 mg/kg will usually cure this. This can be done by administering tetracycline via an eye dropper or by feeding crickets coated with tetracycline powder. With treatment, prognosis is good.

SWOLLEN DIGITS

For obvious reasons, one should avoid chameleons with swollen digits or limbs at the time of purchase. However, swollen digits and limbs will appear in captive animals, frequently during the first few weeks of acclimation following purchase. Without proper tests and cultures the exact causes cannot be determined. Among imports, swollen limbs or digits can result from "crushing" trauma initiated during collecting or packing. One cause that results in a "dry rot" type of syndrome whereby digits initially swell, then turn black and "dry out", is caused by a fungus *(Aspergillus)*. Administration of antibiotics is recommended. After a few days of treatment the swelling often gradually diminishes. Some permanent tissue damage and swelling may result.

Swollen digits can also be the result of bacterial infections. Infected digits will require drainage and antibiotic treatment. In these cases veterinary assistance is definitely recommended but unfortunately prognosis is very questionable.

Female panther chameleon *(Chamaeleo pardalis)* with swollen digits and forelimb. The cause was probably a crushing type of trauma. The animal survived but suffered some permanent damage to the limb.

RESPIRATORY INFECTIONS

How does one know when a chameleon has a respiratory infection? Typical symptoms include periods of slight gaping of mouth, forced exhalations, the presence of an unusual amount of mucus (sometimes slightly bubbly) inside mouth and the distended appearance of the body as if it were swollen with air. Treatment includes raising temperature toward the high range of requirements and treating with injectable antibiotics such as Amikacin® or Baytril® (enrofloxacin). This will require a visit to a veterinarian. Prognosis will depend on several factors including overall health of the animal and the severity of the infection at the time treatment is started.

Prevention

Keeping an animal at appropriate temperatures and providing the opportunity to bask, combined with a diet that offers required vitamins such as vitamin A (via beta-carotene) and vitamin C can significantly help prevent respiratory disorders.

GASTROENTERITIS

This is a general term for gastrointestinal infections. Symptoms usually include diarrhea, weight loss, loss of appetite and, in some cases, blood in the stools. Treatment will require veterinary assistance to determine the causal organism(s) and the appropriate course of treatment. Coccidia, *Entamoeba,* flagelate protozoans *and Salmonella* are common causal agents in true chameleons.